Viz

Roger Mellie's
AD BREAK

B🌳XTREE

First published 2003 by Boxtree
an imprint of Pan Macmillan Publishers Ltd
Pan Macmillan, 20 New Wharf Road, London N1 9RR
Basingstoke and Oxford
Associated companies throughout the world
www.panmacmillan.com

ISBN 0 7522 1553 1

A CIP catalogue record for this book is available from
the British Library.

Printed and bound by The Bath Press

A Foreword by Roger Mellie OBE

When the publishers first approached me with the idea of putting together a book of adverts from 25 years of *Viz Comic,* my first reaction was to tell them to fuck right off.

However, when they explained that my involvement would consist of nothing more strenuous than penning this short introduction in return for an obscenely large cheque, I was only too happy to oblige.

C Wanderbra

PP. R Mellie

5

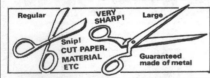

6

Bring back hanging - in the comfort of your own home.
with *NEW* GALLO-MATIC™

5 EASY STEPS

1 2 3 4 5

ALL BRITISH MADE

FROM AROUND **£59**

DESIGN CENTRE AWARD

A **CAPITAL** PRODUCT
Capital Enterprises Ltd. Slough

7

9

COME TO CHURCH

"it's GREAT!"

Christenings

Weddings

Funerals

Jumble Sales

Open Sundays 10am-11.30am. No hats.

Issued by the Vicars Club of Great Britain on behalf of the Churches of England and Wales

10

COME TO PRISON

It's GREAT!

Pop into your local police station and ask for details.

13

The new Satsuma Castanet XR4 Turbo is more than just a car.

It's a fanny magnet.

Drive one and you'll never sleep alone again.

 **Satsuma**

Castanet XR4 Turbo *Fanny Magnet*
You'll have to beat them off with a shitty stick

Satsuma Motor, Lawn Mower and Dangerous Toy Company, Kyoto, Japan.

15

19

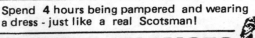

21

THEY'RE HAPPY
Because they eat
LARD

Issued by the Lard Information Council

the Mighty Disciplinarian

Child Beating Machine

Wide range of fully interchangable beating attachments include:

* SLIPPERS
* CANES
* RULERS
* HANDS
* CRICKET BATS
* KNOTTED ROPE
* LEAD PIPES

Potty training in TWO HOURS! No problem! Children quickly learn to fear and respect the Disciplinarian

WARNING! Over zealous use of the Disciplinarian may lead to the death of a child

Torque control allows you to beat a light child from a light tap to within an inch of its life

Fully adjustable. Delivers blows individually or in multiples of six.

SPARE THE ROD AND SPOIL THE CHILD!

Industrial application screw clamp holds the errant child firmly throughout the beating

Will not tire Pity show Pity

'My son checked me. The Disciplinarian took the skin off his arm whilst I had a cup of tea. He hasn't checked me since' Mr. B. Essex

£150 and it's yours!

Armstrong & Titan Punishment Engines, Box 1, Dover

Yes! I am interested in hitting children. Please send me ___ Mighty Disciplinarian Child Beating Machine(s). I enclose a cheque/cash to the value of £.

Name ___ Address ___ Post code ___ Daytime telephone number ___

More machines to be sent - No obligation to buy

Do not tick this box if you would not prefer to decline to not not refuse to not not not NOT agree to accept that we may flog your personal details to any fucking crackpot who wants a go at getting his hands on some of your cash ☐

Come to Middlesbrough
and smell our fumes

A Fortnight in Cleveland's Petrochemical Wonderland costs from as little as £4...

Kit-e-Mince

DON'T WASTE YOUR MONEY ON EXPENSIVE DOGFOOD!

Feed your dog the way NATURE intended...

2 minced cats a day provide your dog with everything he needs to keep him in tip-top condition - with healthy teeth and bones, a glossy coat and a shiny nose.

£39.99 from shops

Larger dogs may require more minced cats.

LEARN DENTISTRY No Joke
By Mail *In Five Hours*

Turn Your Talent Into Money

SEND ONE PENNY
E.FRYMIRE

"I went out on a job last night after school, from which I made £300" E.FRYMIRE PENNY

Get back on your feet from just £39*

It's everyone's nightmare. You're walking alone at night in an unfamiliar area and your shoes suddenly break down. What do you do? Attempt to repair them yourself? Abandon your footwear on the pavement and struggle home in your socks? Well, now there's a third option. National Shoe Breakdown rescue service.

Membership of **NATIONAL SHOE BREAKDOWN** entitles you to:

● **Pathside assistance.** Trained cobblers on call 24 hours a day, 7 days a week. Over 85% of breakdowns fixed on the spot whether its a loose heel, snapped lace, flapping sole or something in your shoe.

● **Complete cover,** even when you're wearing someone else's footwear. You're the member, not the shoes.

● **Priority** to members in vulnerable situations, such as lone women who have trod in a dog turd.

● **Relay service.** If the fault cannot be rectified on the pavement we'll get you and your shoes to your destination.

● **Replacement footwear.** If your shoes cannot be repaired within 24 hours, we'll provide courtesy flip flops for up to 7 days.

● **HOMESTART.** Can't find one of your slippers in the morning? Our qualified shoesmiths will be round to look under the sofa, or retrieve it from the dog's mouth.

To join, call us **now** on
0000 994 388
Calls cost 95p per minute cheap rate

*£39 is the cost of standard cover which does not include RELAY or HOMESTART and may not apply to certain high performance shoes such as hand-stiched Italian pigskin brogues or crocodile loafers.

Line up! Line up! Experience some of the most EXCITING queues you will EVER stand in!

50 YEARS of QUEUES

1971 to 2001

Queue Gardens
Amusement Park

Get Wet 'n' Wild standing in the THRILLING AquaQueue!

NEW THIS YEAR! The Spectacular meandering CorksQueue

One ticket gets you in - then all the queuing is **FREE!**

We DARE you to wait in the 'White Knuckle Line' - the longest queue of its type in Europe

Free queuing for up to **1000 cars**

PLEASE NOTE- You may have to wait to stand in some of the more popular queues at peak times and Bank Holidays

HULL

QUEUE GARDENS ▪

A158

MILFORD HAVEN

Queue Gardens
- where the excitement never begins

Please note - Queue Gardens appologises that following an incident where several people died of boredom, the Fortress of Tedium Queue is closed until safety checks can be carried out.

YOU CAN'T MISS WITH

ARMITAGE SHANKS

Is it a *telly*? Is it a *shed*? It's *neither*, yet it's BOTH! It's a

TellyShed

Colour or Black and White

Telly or Shed. *YOU* decide.

£199

Become a **MILLIONAIRE** in 3 WEEKS Making MONEY from **MICE!**

"I bought a mouse. Three weeks later I was a MILLIONAIRE!"
Mr. B., Essex

Send 30p for a mouse to Millionaire Mouse Farms, Wales

"The other day I played chess with Mr Kipling. 'What an exceedingly good chess set', I mused".

For over a hundred years families have enjoyed Mr Kipling's cakes. Now, the excellence of those cakes has been captured for ever in a superb commemorative chess set, crafted in the finest marble and alabaster, a fitting tribute to the man and his cakes.

To Cherish and enjoy

Every piece in this set has been expertly sculpted and detailed making it a pleasure to pick up, and a joy to behold. This is truly a chess set to cherish and enjoy. A chess set that Mr Kipling himself would be proud to own.

The board is in itself a work of art. Hand carved from carefully selected pieces of former Brazilian rain forest, this immaculate hardwood base doubles as a carrying case and provides a fitting home for these unique cake chess pieces.

Accompanying the set is a fascinating booklet that charts the history of Mr Kipling cakes, and introduces each piece in turn. From the Bramley Apple Pie pawns, obediently standing in line, ready to make the greatest sacrifice a Kipling cake can make. To the gallant knights, hewn in the form of the classic Jam Tart. Ever popular, ever true. A battle proud warrior, fit to lead his army of courageous cakes. Each piece an individual cake, with its own qualities, its own strengths. Together they form an invincible army of cake.

Affordably low price

The Mister Kipling Cake Chess Set is available exclusively by subscription from the Trebor Mint. Subscribers will receive one piece each month at an affordably low price of only £96.50. What's more, the board and information booklet are yours free, for a one off payment of only £29.99.

THE
🌿 MR 🌿
KIPLING
CHESS SET

Magnificently detailed, fine marble and alabaster sculptures. Capturing for all eternity the beauty and elegance of Mr Kipling's cakes.

This will be a limited edition set, an heirloom quality work of art that is guaranteed to appreciate in value with the passage of years, and we therefore urge you to subscribe NOW to avoid disappointment.

This is a rare opportunity to own a chess set that will not only excite devotees of the game, but also one that will delight anyone interested in Mr Kipling's cakes.

The King – represented by the Bakewell Slice, truly the ruler of the cake Kingdom. A masterpiece among Mr Kipling cakes. Standing proud behind a shield of icing, he sits atop his double thrown, crafted in the powerful image of the foil cake cup. Majestically the King surveys his army.

Shown smaller than actual size.

The Bishop. With deserved respect our artist has chosen to represent this piece with the Fondant Fancy. Sitting either side of his King and Queen, the Bishop, resplendent in his fluted paper case, brings dignity and humanity to the game.

The Rook. Sturdy and solid, he signifies strength, as represented by Mr Kipling's Jaffa Finger. One of the most popular of Mr Kipling's cakes, the detailing of this piece simply has to be seen to be believed.

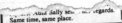

27

Rievaulx Abbey plc

MONK
£21~30k (pro rata) depending on age and experience.

Hours~ 168 pw

We are an established monastery looking to appoint a highly motivated and experienced monk to run and expand our team of brethren.
The successful applicant will demonstrate:

* *Strong chanting skills*
* *Proven track record in wandering around cloisters*
* *Ability to keep bees under pressure*

If this is you and you're looking to join one of Britain's most dynamic and challenging closed communities, e-mail **dominic47@cofe.com** or write enclosing your cv and details of your current package to:
Brother Dominic, Personnel and Recruitment Unit, Rievaulx Abbey, North Yorkshire.

Closing date for applications
30th June 2002.   Quote Ref V1

*Rievaulx Abbey-
Buzzin'* R**T**A

You cannot whack a tab!

Mount Grace Priory

mount grace priory

Monk - £30K + sandals

MGP *is seeking a dynamic and experienced Monk to work as part of a team drawing and illuminating large capital letters to tight deadlines.*

The successful applicant will be a self starter with excellent sitting quiet skills and a proven ability to say nothing for years on end. A sound knowledge of gazing heaven-enward with the fingertips together is essential.

For further information and a job application pack, log onto www.mountgracepriory.com/monks or contact Brother Maynard, Human Resources Manager, Mount Grace Priory, Ripon.

Monk £35k + frugal fare +relocation package

The Brothers of Canterbury Ltd

are seeking to recruit a highly motivated and ambitious monk with a strong and proven track record of not touching his own genitals to head a team of novices. The appointee will be required to plan and implement long term cross platform prayer strategies.

If you have:
* *At least 5 years experience of loving the Lord at senior level*
* *A positive approach to working as part of a team droning in Latin*
* *The drive and vision to work in a dynamic non-communicating Trappist environment*
* *A pious attitute towards life*

Then **WE** want to hear from **YOU!**

Send a cv along with the name address of two referees to: The Brothers of Canterbury Ltd, Canterbury Priory, Canterbury.

St. Peter's Monastery

Saint Peter's Monastery

**MONK (residential)
50k pa + bonus**

St. Peter's is a creative, dynamic and successful monastery founded in 1232. Following restructuring we are looking to recruit a confident and enthusiastic go-getting monk who would fit in with our highly motivated professional performance management framework team.

Building upon our existing business base, maintaining and strengthening our partnership agenda and maximising our mead production are the three key strategic priorities for this exciting and demanding role.

The successful applicant will have a clear commitment to growing herbs, getting up at three in the morning and bell ringing, combined with sound experience of living off porridge. A small bald patch on the top your head would also be an advantage.

*St. Peter's Monastery ~
"achieving progress
through quiet reflection"*

PRONTOMONK
Monk Temping Agency

At PRONTO Monk Temping Agency, we can help with all your staff problems. Whether you need one monk for half a day or a full order for a year, we can provide the monks to cover any eventuality. All our personnel have full calligraphic, chanting and bee keeping skills and are available at short notice.

Whatever your order requirement, PRONTOMONK Temping Agency can provide it~

- •**Benedictines**
- •**Dominicans** •**Carmelites**
- •**Gregorians** •**Franciscans**
- •**Carthusians** •**Trappists**
- •**Cistercians**

Call 0802 222 33 or visit our website at www.prontomonk.com

"You'll thank Heaven for PRONTOMONK!"

Problems sorting mice from rats?

The Vermifuge
does it all at the flick of a switch

We've got **Vermifuges** to suit all pockets- from table top models to semi-industrial. Drop us a line and we'll advise on the right Vermifuge for **YOU!**

Piper Rodent Sorting Systems, Box 1, Hamlyn.

The Egyptians knew the secret of LONG HAIR

Now *YOU* can too with 'Pyramid' formula mystical growth

HAIR COMPOST

Your hair will simply grow and grow!

- **NO MORE BALD PATCHES!**
- **GROW THICK BLACK LOCKS OVERNIGHT!**

This million year old formula has been carved on pyramid walls and passed down through the centuries by the Egyptian mystical Kings. Now the head compost of the ancients can be yours for as little as £79.99 a sack.

WARNING
Do not wear motorcycle helmet within 2 hours of compost application as rapid hair growth will occur.

APPLY DAILY TO THE TOP OF YOUR HEAD IN A DARKENED ROOM, THEN LIE DOWN WITH YOUR ARMS FOLDED FOR HALF AN HOUR. SIMPLE AS THAT. AND WITHIN MINUTES YOU WILL HAVE STRONG, THICK, HEALTHY SHOULDER LENGTH BLACK HAIR.

MANNING · 2 · MANNING

"I'M NO RACIST, I T*KE THE PISS OUT THE PUFFS TOO"
000 5435 4342

"I'VE GOT FUCKING D*AB*TES, ME"
000 7567 7657

"REMEMBER, L**K AFTER YOUR FUCKIN' M*THER"
000 7567 7657

calls cost the same as shares in ICI and terminate in their underpants in a chair surrounded by chintz and bric-a-brac

NOW *THAT'S* WHAT I CALL SHOUTING

Lord Tonypandy Shouts... Order! Order!

ORDER! ORDER!

Double CD or Cassette Over 2 hours of the very best cries of Order! Order! from Britain's best loved Speaker of the House

Turn YOUR speakers of the House full up and listen to all your favourites, including-

*Order! Order!
*Order! Order!..Order!
*Orrrrrrder! ORDER!!
-and many more

Recorded live at the House of Commons

Out Now on Tonypandymonium Records. Order! Order! your copy Today!

EX-TOASTER ENGINEER REVEALS UNKNOWN SECRETS!!

Would 100 slices of toast a day, EVERY day, make a difference to you? In this highly acclaimed book an ex-toaster engineer reveals all the latest pop-up tricks you need to make any toaster cough up toast again and again! Most of what you will read is not published in the toaster manuals!

The book They tried to BAN!

Which machines to use and when **The secrets** of the Browning button. **Toasting** cycles- once you're making toast, how to keep making it This book describes the method used by engineers to test the toasters, and by using it you can empty any toaster in minutes. It's amazingly simple and works on nearly every toaster made within the last three years.

"We made 180 slices of toast in one hour using this guide" -GQ Magazine

29

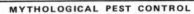

...atar... ...vities in the village.

Are the squares hassling you for bread?

Hey. Chill out.

If there's one thing you don't need at college, it's hassle. Like the landlord causing a heavy scene about the rent. Or you've checked out a groovy pair of strides in a hip boutique, but you ain't got no moolar to buy them with. And you can't do your homework, cos you used your last sheet of paper rolling up a bong to smoke happy baccy.

On top of all these problems the last thing you need is a wrinkly dude bank manager who hassles you the minute your account goes a couple of 'K' O.D.

At Berkleys we understand about student life. All of our managers used to be students back in the thirties. We know that you need more than pens, pencils and protractors to see you through the term. You also need chewing gum, pop records, cinema tickets and fizzy drinks. And after a hard day's work you wanna hang out with the other cats in the Union bar, or maybe buy tickets to see the latest pop group.

At Berkleys, that's cool. Our staff are all hip to the jive, daddy oh. And we aren't going to lay some heavy guilt trip on you just cos you go a couple of grand into the red. Like, big deal. It's only bread, yeah? At your local branch you'll find all of our staff are hip cats, just like you. In fact, don't be surprised if you see our Student Advice Officer in the local record shop checking out the latest sounds. So why not come and check **us** out, or complete the coupon below and collect a free* pencil sharpener, Biro pen and a packet of chewing gum.

Come into our parlour...

Berkleys Student Bank Account · (Complete coupon in BLOCK CAPITALS)

Dear Mr Spider,

I am a fly. Please may I come into your parlour. Send me details of Berkleys Student Accounts.

Name .... Address..

.... Post code..............................

BERKLEYS

Cuddly Toy or Ursine Maniac - YOU decide.

The Detritus Gallery proudly presents

Little Ted West

The first in a brand new limited edition collectors' series

'Bears of Murder'

*S*ince 1994, the mere mention of 25 Cromwell Street has struck terror into the hearts of the British public. For in that year a horrified nation held its breath and placed bets on the final total as the so-called house of horrors gave up its hideous secrets. For this was the infamous address where illiterate murderer Fred West killed and disposed of his hapless victims, plastering their rotting corpses into the walls and entombing them under the floors.

We must never forget his chilling reign of evil. And what better way to remember the homicidal Gloucester pervert than with this heirloom collector bear - 'Little Ted West'?

The first in a limited edition series, Little Ted stands a murderous eight inches high. With his yokel's tank top and his mop of curly hair, who would guess that beneath his fluffy exterior beats the cold heart of a notorious rapist, torturer and serial killer? The real Fred cheated justice by hanging himself before he could stand trial. But for just one payment of £29.95* Little Ted will stand trial - on your mantelpiece, helping you to trawl your mind for vividly-imagined details of his many vile atrocities.

Little Ted West is both a charming memento of one man's dark and sadistic odyssey of stomach-turning sexual violence, and a disturbingly malevolent evocation of pure whimsy.

Not actual price.

Apply for Little Ted West and receive swastika lunatic Little Ted Manson on approval. We will send you a different Bear of Murder every month until our craftsmen run out of murderers to do bears of.

I am both repulsed yet strangely aroused by true-life tales of murder and dismemberment like you get in those Marshall Cavendish part-works. I particularly like sitting on the toilet, peering at those those grainy black and white photographs of chopped-up bodies in trunks until I can make out a distinct severed hand or foot. This has been the only outlet for my morbid voyeurism until now. It's just possible these Bears of Murder may pull me back from the brink of turning into the next Dennis Nielsen. Then again, they may merely take my mental pathology to a whole new level. Please send me **Little Ted West**. I enclose a vast quantity of money.

Name _____

Address _____ Post Code _____

Little Ted West comes with a certificate bearing the signature mark of the artist, Herman Jelmet, and the brother-in-law of the milkman of the Assistant Deputy Chief Constable of Gloucestershire.

Herman Jelmet

NAZI CARAVAN

incorporating *EXTREME RIGHT-WING MOTORHOME*

£3.60

Issue 112   August 2001

INCREASE YOUR LEBENSRAUM
move up to a 6 berth this summer

HEIL HITCHER
the final solution in tow bars

MEIN KAMPFSITE
Professor David Irving takes us to his favourite spot

AWNINGS
the simplest way to annex your neighbour's pitch

ARYAN SPACIOUS
we review the *Panzer Pirouette* the first caravan to be awarded 5 yellow stars

REICH OF WAY
motoring tips for travel abroad

ON SALE NOW

QUACKING GOOD VALUE!

CHOOSE any 5 from only 50p each (+ p&p)

1. RRP £16.99 Offer price £1.00
2. RRP £14.99 Offer price £1.00 — BLUE EGGS
3. RRP £10.99 Offer price 50p
4. RRP £29.99 Offer price £2.00
5. RRP £22.99 Offer price £2.00 — COUNTS AS ONE CHOICE
6. RRP £16.99 Offer price £1.00
7. RRP £16.99 Offer price £1.00
8. RRP £14.99 Offer price £1.00
9. RRP £20.99 Offer price £1.50 — COUNTS AS ONE CHOICE
10. RRP £29.95 Offer price £2.50
11. RRP £9.99 Offer price 50p — SEXUALLY EXPLICIT
12. RRP £15.99 Offer price £1.00
13. RRP £14.98 Offer price £1.00
14. RRP £11.99 Offer price £1.00 — FEATHERBACK EDITION
15. RRP £9.99 Offer price 50p
16. RRP £17.99 Offer price £1.50
17. RRP £14.97 Offer price £1.00
18. RRP £12.99 Offer price £1.00 — WEBBED FEET
19. RRP £15.98 Offer price £1.50 — POINTY ARSE
20. RRP £11.99 Offer price 50p
21. RRP £11.99 Offer price 50p
22. RRP £11.99 Offer price 50p
23. RRP £25.00 Offer price £2.50 — COUNTS AS ONE CHOICE

To: Duck of the Month Club,
PO Box 50, Slimbridge, Glos.

Please accept my application and enrol me as a member of the Duck of the Month Club and send me the 5 introductory birds whose numbers I have indicated in the boxes provided. I will be charged only the special introductory offer prices, plus a total of £1.65 towards postage and packing. As a member, I will receive approximately every month (ie. every other day) a free Duck of the Month Club magazine. I understand that the quality of the Ducks offered in these magazines will spiral downwards as sharply as their price rockets upwards, and I will inevitably find myself buying large quantities of unwanted ducks that I cannot afford and will never look at. My only obligation is to buy everything from these magazines, and that the minimum length of membership is for the rest of my natural life. If after this period I wish to cancel, I can do so by giving one month's notice in writing.

Membership is subject to acceptance. We may consult a sinister credit reference agency to see how deeply and for how long we can shaft your arse.

Name.....................
Address.....................
....
Signed.....................

Duck of the Month Club
Quacking Value

AT LAST! A DIFFERENT KIND OF DUCK CLUB!

A club that promises you the best and very latest ducks at a fraction of high street prices. From the best-selling Buff Orpington and Miniature Appleyard to the classic Khaki Campbell and Welsh Harlequin. From the Lavish East Indian Drake and Abacot Ranger to the spicy Blue Swedish and Chocolate Runner, you're sure to find what you are looking for in Britain's largest Duck Club.

MEMBERSHIP HAS ITS REWARDS

Our buyers ensure that the selection of waterfowl we offer is the latest and best, and all our ducks carry huge discounts - of up to 40% off duck shop prices.

SELECT YOUR DUCKS NOW

To become a member of the Duck of the Month Club, simply choose any 5 of the superb items shown here from ONLY 50 PENCE EACH! (+ p&p) but SEND NO MONEY NOW. We invite you to examine the ducks in your own home for 10 days before you decide to keep them. Should you choose not to keep them, simply twist their necks, return them to us, your membership will be cancelled and you will owe nothing.

The Experience of a Lifetime

15 DAYS: 29 APRIL - 13 MAY 1997

MON 29th APRIL *Drive to Hull in beige Morris Marina which has done 412 miles since new.* **TUES 30th** *Morning sitting on boat whilst they try to start the engines* **WED 1st MAY** *Arrive at Goole for visit to Copper Kettle Tea Rooms where Tupperware will be on sale.* **THURS 2nd** *Arrive Grimsby. Minibus excursion to Tetney Post Office to pick up pensions.* **FRI 3rd** *Morning rounding Spurn Head.* **SAT 4th** *At sea.* **SUN 5th** *At sea. Ship springs diesel leak.* **MON 6th** *Drifting helplessly in the Hull-Oslo Ferry lane. Spectacular early morning near miss with Copenhagen Ferry.* **TUES 7th** *Arrive Redcar. Disembark for non-optional Quayside*

C ruise in style amidst a sea of Tupperware on the Tupperware Viking's maiden voyage

The quest for the dream holiday for lovers of practical, stylish and economical kitchen storage ends aboard the Tupperware Viking. As you enter the twilight of your life, Twilight Years Cruise Company present a once in a lifetime golden opportunity to set sail on that luxury cruise you've always dreamed of, as we invite you to shuffle aboard our magnificently converted factory ship for her maiden voyage around the Humber estuary, discovering new worlds of Tupperware.

TAKE YOUR ENFEEBLED MIND ON A VOYAGE OF DISCOVERY

Your holiday begins at Hull docks, where you'll be given a cup of tea and a nice sit down. The staff and crew of the Tupperware Viking will be there to help you with the stairs when it's time to board the floating five star hotel that is to be your home for the next two weeks.

You'll feel instantly at home in your cosy, windowless cabin, thoughtfully ensconced deep in the bowels of the ship, close to the warmth and comforting drone of the engine room.

RELAX IN THE COMFORT AND STYLE OF A BYGONE AGE

Time has little meaning aboard the Tupperware Viking. Your days are your own, whether you choose to spend them in the ship's own tea room, or relaxing under a tarpaulin on the sleet deck, drinking in the magnificent vistas of the North Sea. The ship has been specially designed with the mature passenger in mind. For instance, no matter where you are, you're never more than 50 metres from a lavatory.

There's even a coroner on board to ensure that the death of a loved one need not mean the end of your holiday. Burials at sea can be arranged with an absolute minimum of fuss and paperwork.

BUT MOST OF ALL, THERE'S THE TUPPERWARE

Each new dawn will bring a myriad of exciting Tupperware activities to choose from. The ship's Tupperware shop is open 24 hours a day for the sale of your favourite modular freezer-safe plastics at rock bottom prices. There's regular Tupperware displays and exhibitions, and our eminent speakers will guide you through an enlightening journey of Tupperware discovery. There's also a convenient trolley service, allowing you to buy Tupperware in the comfort of your own cabin.

WE'LL ENTERTAIN YOU IN BODY AND MIND

On the cruise will be Professor Abel J. Cribb, former Principal Tupperwarologist at Bournemouth Kelloggs University, who will share his expertise in talks aboard and excursions ashore. And other eminent speakers will guide you through the exciting and intriguing world of flexible, lifetime guaranteed food storage systems. Each evening's talk is followed by a lively Tupperware Party, where you can dance to the Tupperware Band, and buy more Tupperware.

POSSIBLY YOUR LAST CHANCE TO EXPERIENCE THIS SPECIAL TUPPERWARE HOLIDAY

None of us are getting any younger, and let's face it - you can't take it with you. Prices for the "Tupperware Cruise" start from £15,995 per person (that's about a mattress full). Price includes cup of tea and a sit down at Hull. All food and Tupperware are extra. A 10% discount is available for the geriatrically disorientated. Book now, before you die. Fill in the coupon today.

GUEST SPEAKERS

PROFESSOR ABEL J. CRIBB
'What Price Food Freshness?'

ROSS DAVIDSON *Star of Eastenders*
'Storage of Cooked and Raw Meats'

RICHARD BAKER *Former BBC Newsreader and pensioner's friend.*
'From Tin to Tupperware! The history of the sandwich box'

TV GLADIATOR 'SHADOW'
'Breakfast Breakthrough - Keeping cereals crunchy the Tupperware way'

DAME THORA HIRD
'A Life in the Theatre (with Tupperware)'

Tupperware Market. **WED 8th** *At sea. Small fire in engine room. Night spent on deck avoiding thick smoke.* **THURS 9th** *Towed into Teesport by slurry barge. Minibus excursion to Yarm Post Office to pick up pensions.* **FRI 10th** *At sea. Ship listing badly. Appears to be going in circles.* **SAT 11th** *Arrive Teesport again. Optional excursion to view magnificent fire at major petrochemical factory.* **SUN 12th** *Set sail for Hull. Relaxing day at sea. Captains farewell Tupperware Dinner in the evening.* **MON 13th** *Ship runs aground on Kilnsea sand flats. Transfer by Bosun's Chair to minibus.* **TUES 14th** *Minibus runs into ditch in Partringham. Unscheduled overnight stay in minibus in ditch.* **WED 15th** *Arrive at Hull Docks car park 48 hours late. Beige Marina stolen.*

600 years of aesthetic femininity

FOR CENTURIES, the World's great artists have drawn their inspiration from women's tits. From Leonardo to Picasso, from Rembrandt to Rolf Harris, knockers have been one of the enduring themes to which the creative genius has returned time and again.

Now, the Royal Male invites you to join in celebrating 600 years of churns in art. Our new portfolio of postage stamps features some of the most beautiful and timeless headlamps selected from the greatest paintings in the World's most magnificent collections. They're yours to cherish in the privacy of your own lavatory for years to come.

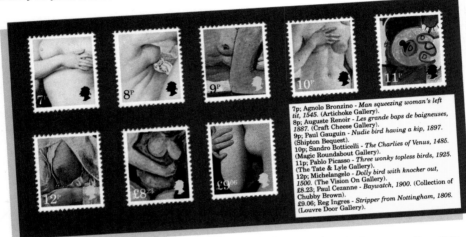

7p; Agnolo Bronzino - *Man squeezing woman's left tit,* 1545. (Artichoke Gallery).
8p; Auguste Renoir - *Les grande baps de baigneuses,* 1887. (Craft Cheese Gallery).
9p; Paul Gauguin - *Nudie bird having a kip,* 1897. (Shipton Bequest).
10p; Sandro Botticelli - *The Charlies of Venus,* 1485. (Magic Roundabout Gallery).
11p; Pablo Picasso - *Three wonky topless birds,* 1925. (The Tate & Lyle Gallery).
12p; Michelangelo - *Dolly bird with knocker out,* 1500. (The Vision On Gallery).
£8.23; Paul Cezanne - *Baywatch,* 1900. (Collection of Chubby Brown).
£9.06; Reg Ingres - *Stripper from Nottingham,* 1806. (Louvre Door Gallery).

Available November 1st from your Post Office, Newsagent or Mucky Bookshop

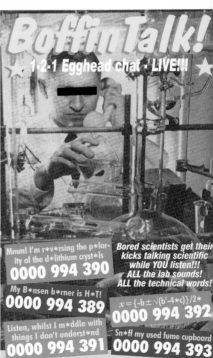

A dental tribute to
HRH Queen Elizabeth the Queen Mother
32 *Glorious* Teeth

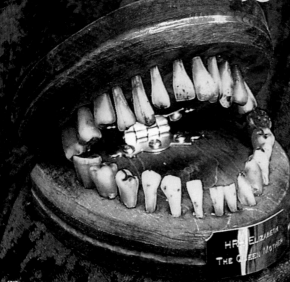

*F*or 99 years, HRH The Queen mother has been the nation's favourite granny. For nearly a century she has selflessly waved, accepted countless bunches of flowers and tirelessly been whisked off to the races in one of her six Rolls Royces. And she has asked for nothing in return, except for several castles and millions of pounds of our money, tax free.

She has many loves - among them horses, choking on fish-bones and gin . But it is her radiant browny-yellow smile that has earned her a special place in the hearts of the nation.

The Old Bag of Hearts

It is a smile that has never flagged, even through the dark days of the blitz. Now we at the Rumpole and Bailey galleries have commissioned a breathtaking set of dental sculptures that will bring the majesty of her teeth to your humble mantlepiece. Crafted of finest quality Montevideo porcelain by world renowned 'tooth artist' Pedro Vagina, each sculture is meticulously hand manked so that every stain and area of decaying enamel is precisely deliniated.

The People's Crone

Month by month, you will receive these exquisite sculptures that will build into a collection anyone like you would be proud to own. And with your first Royal Tooth, you will receive completely free of no extra charge this magnificent pair of mahogany gums, the ideal way to display your collection in all its grandure.

The Royal upper inscisor- displaying authentic chips acquired whilst biting through a swan at a garden party in 1953.

The Royal second molar- part of HRH The Queen Mother's dental landscape since it first appeared in1907.

BASED ON A TRUE STORY

Christmas 1987. At around 8.15pm on Thursday 24th December, 72 year old Edward Wilson died alone at his home in Thornaby, Cleveland, the victim of hypothermia.

Ten days later the fairy lights on his Christmas tree failed. After two months 'Ping!' The light bulb went. A fortnight later and the standard lamp conked out too.

Six months on and a fuse in Mr Wilson's fridge blew. The contents, already green with mould, began to stink. Not long afterwards mice gnawing at the wires rendered the telephone inoperative. After ten months the doorbell batteries ran flat. And twelve months after his death even Mr Wilson's wristwatch had ground to a halt.

But FOUR YEARS later, long after the maggots had picked him dry, Mr Wilson's **SAMSUN** TV was still working. And as the police officers who found the body discovered, the colour was still as bright as ever.

SAMSUN
televisions
Guaranteed for life. And beyond...

33

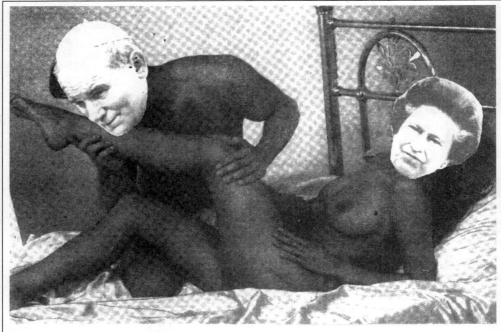

BENETTON Jumpers from £25.99

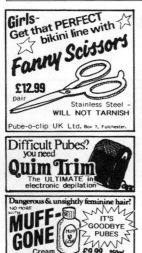

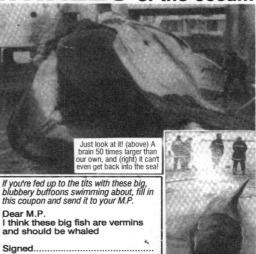
35

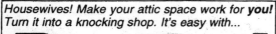

36

37

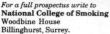

38

39

ADVERTISMENT

'PLAY IN A DAY' with the
NEW MAESTROMATIC
from Ron-Tel

IDEAL GIFT

only **£6.99** WAS £119.99

YOU'LL BE THE LIFE AND SOUL OF THE PARTY

From all good record shops, chemists and major branches of WHSmiths

---

OLD LADIES

If you don't pay your gas bill this winter

YOU'RE GOING TO PRISON

The Gas Board
We'll get our fucking bit – don't you worry

You get a higher quality turd blocking the toilet when you travel

FIRST CLASS

British Rail First Class
Same train. Same hold ups. Different price

41

Ladies! *Nip Tumescence in the Bud...with the*

SEXUAL TEMPERANCE SPOON

Guaranteed to soften even the most optimistic ardour!

SCHOOL nurses have known for centuries that a sharp blow from a cold spoon is the best way to tame an unwelcome erection. Now at last, these spoons are available to the public. If you finished with all that nonsense twenty years ago, but it still raises its ugly head, then this spoon is for YOU!

ONE WHACK AND IT'S ON THE SLACK!

Stop it before *he* starts!

Made in Sheffield from finest quality stainless steel, the Sexual Temperance Spoon is kept nice and cold in its own miniature chilling cabinet. Measuring only 6ins x 6ins x 10ins, the cabinet fits easily on the bedside table, ready for any nocturnal emergency.

"My hubby got ideas one night after watching 'Carry On Camping'. A quick flick with the Temperance Spoon sent him scampering to the spare room with his tail between his legs. Thanks!" **Mrs. R Barnsley**

"It's a SPOON!" **Mrs. B Essex**

It's the only spoon that STOPS stirring!

only £24.99 from all good shops

Please note: *Extremely turgid erections may require more than one whack on the lid.*

'Down, Boy' Chastity Products. Unit 6. Fulchester Industrial Estate. Leeds

43

Turn WATER into PETROL
WITH
Petrol Fish™
THE FISH THAT (Esso) TRIED TO BAN!

- *Fuel bills vanish overnight!*
- *Beat price increases at the PUMPS!*
- *Enjoy FREE motoring FOR LIFE!*

These rare and only recently discovered goldfish occur naturally deep beneath the Earth in the oil fields of Saudi Arabia. No larger than ordinary goldfish, and the same colour, their unique bio-chemistry gives them an unusually high octane capacity. As a result when they drink water, their urine turns into petrol. Place just one of these fish in your petrol tank then fill it with water and within seconds nature's miraculous **PETROL FISH** are turning the water into petrol. So successful is this natural fuel saving technique lawyers from all the major petrol companies have tried to ban the sale of our product. So far they have been unsuccessful, but we recommend that you ORDER TODAY while **PETROL FISH** are still legally available.

Please rush me................*(state quantity) **PETROL FISH** @£100 each.

Name................................Address................................

Tick one ☐FOUR STAR ☐UNLEADED ☐SUPER PLUS UNLEADED.

*Sorry we regret that customers are limited to a maximum of 800 fish each.

Send orders to: PETROL FISH SALES (UK) Ltd., The Aquarium, Colchester High Street, Colchester, Essex, CO1 5AH.

JOIN THE ARMY

COS ALL THE BIRDS ARE
GAGGING FOR SQUADDIES

If you aren't getting any, then Britain's modern army is the place to be. After 6 months' basic training your shoulders will be broad, and your knob will be red raw with shagging. So if you fancy a bit, pop in to your local recruiting office or fill in the form for more details.

To: The Army, Aldershot

I'm not getting my end away and I reckon 33 years hiding behind some garden wall in Belfast will just about see me right.

Name _____ Address _____

_____

_____

51

52

Iss. 26. vol. 45   October 2000 £2.50

BIG

Incorporating **Dairy Angler**

CHEESE

.00lb
abybel landed
n Suffolk. *picture p.30*

The magazine for people who think you catch cheese in the sea

Landing a 10lb Stilton-
The experts tell you how

**Port Salut
- which
bait to
use to
hook a
monster**

Sea-Edam - *An elusive
summer visiter to our shores*

**Win a week
tickling
Jarlesbergs
in the ffjords
of Norway**

Fly Fishing for Soft Cheeses
- how to double your catch

LOOKING FOR A NEW BRIE ROD?
-WE PUT FIVE OF THE BEST TO THE TEST

On sale NOW

Get into her knickers with Interflower.

With bouquets starting at only £10,
there's no better way to get your fingers and tops.

54

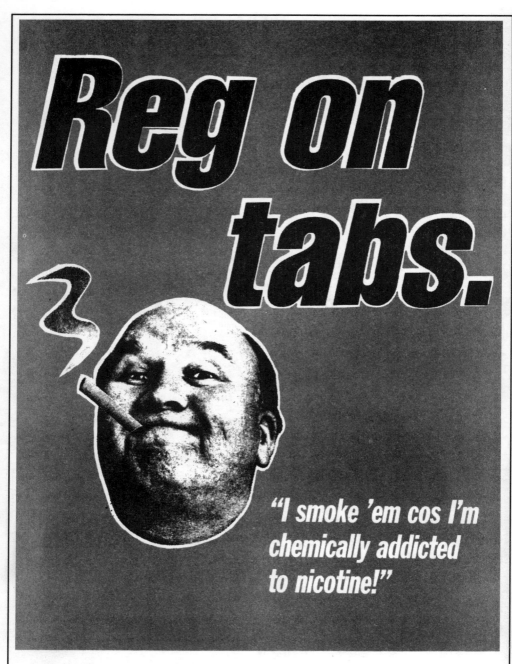

WARNING: SMOKING WHILST PREGNANT CAN
LEAD TO LOW BIRTH WEIGHT. MIND YOU, WHO
WANTS TO GIVE BIRTH TO A FAT BABY ANYWAY.
Health Department's Chief Medical Officers

57

"Tap your way to stardom, like me!" says the late FRED ASTAIRE.

FRED ASTAIRE'S TAP-o-MATIC

AUTOMATIC DANCE TRAINING ENGINE

VARIABLE RHYTHMS from a soothing soft-shoe-shuffle up to a frenzied flamenco at over *600* beats *per second!*

SIMPLY BOLT Tap-O-Matic's dancing pistons onto your shoes, press the starter, adjust the tempo control, and you're away!

INCLUDED FREE! If you reply within seven days, receive a bonus parcel containing Lambada and Foxtrot overdrive cogs and Disco turbocharger attachment!!

Only £899.99

A REALSTIC moulded plastic Fred Astaire head barks out dancing instructions in time with your chosen music.

Remember - Consult your doctor before fastening your feet to ANY petrol-powered dancing machine.

Dear the late FRED ASTAIRE, Please send me ___ TAP-O-MATIC Dancing Engines. I enclose cheque/ Postal order made payable to "The Late Fred Astaire Company of Great Britain Ltd" for _____ NAME CAPITALS PLEASE ___ ADDRESS___ POSTAL CODE_

ORDER NOW TO GUARANTEE DELIVERY BEFORE CHRISTMAS We regret that orders at this extra special rate must be limited to a maximum of 25 Tap-o-matic Dancing Engines per household

SEND TO; *TAP-O-MATIC INDUSTRIES* Inc. Suite 44378, *45,642 West 95th and Main, Chicago, Illinois, New Orleans Idaho New York State, USA, Zip code 1*

59

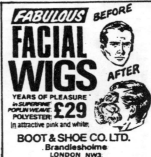

61

63

Not got the bottle to buy a jazzmag...?

Primary school halfway
up a fucking mountain?
No problem.

STOP
CHILDREN

The Satsuma Mohican

The Satsuma Mohican is a unique 4x4 that will take any terrain in its stride. From the traffic-calming measures outside the nursery school, to that pot-hole in Sainsbury's car park, nothing gets in its way. Its revolutionary low-ratio five-speed transfer box and limited-slip differential make short work of the steepest multi-storey, whilst its double wishbone suspension and rugged ladder chassis make child's play of mounting the kerb to use the cashpoint. And when the going gets rough, the Mohican passes the McDonalds Drive-Thru test with ease, thanks to its 6 litre V8 engine and featherlight power steering. The Satsuma Mohican- take it anywhere, but not too far from a petrol station. Call **005690 6151**

SATSUMA
SLEDGEHAMMERS TO CRACK NUTS

Satsuma Mohican £31,200 on the road. Price includes child seats, driver side vanity mirror, handbag compartment, dashboard jamrag holder, hands-free lipstick applicator, Chris Rea CD, number plates and delivery. Warranty 3 years or 400 miles. Model shown Satsuma Mohican Geronimo £50,500

'Tragic Memories'
Classic Collectables
TOP QUALITY DIE CAST MODELS

Combine the joy of reading the world's dirtiest bongo mags with the pride of owning them in the most luxurious editions.

100 of the best Scud Magazines ever printed

NEW CUNTS

Yours for only £8.99

Timeless Masterpieces for the Discerning Masturbator

We all like to surround ourselves with beautiful and elegant things ~ Champagne, antique oil paintings and wafer-thin chocolates all stand as a testimony to our good taste and discernment. But are you let down by your tatty stash of spangle mags?

The Wanklyn Print are proud to offer you the chance to own a pornographic library that would not be out of place in any stately home.

You only have to hold these volumes in your left hand to appreciate the artistry that goes into the creation of each one. From the supple leather spine lavishly decorated in 55 carrot gold, to the paper, specially milled to reduce porn glare, you'll experience the joy of gently leafing through this classic grumble collection .

Accept 'New Cunts' for the introductory price of £8.99 (regular price £34.99), and we'll send you a new classic title each week for your approval. We're sure you'll want to keep each volume, but if you decide not to, simply return it to us unsoiled and wait for the next one to come. New Cunts is yours to wank over whatever you decide.

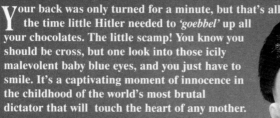

Very few discerning people will ever own *The Life of Christ in Cats*

The life story of Jesus,
gloriously captured in cats by
internationally reviled Birthday
Card artist Antonio Fictitio.
Crafted in the finest *Armitage Shanks Urinal Grade Porcelain*.

Artist - Antonio Fictitio
(shown smaller than actual size of 4'11")

It is the greatest story ever told. A man whose life brought joy and hope to the faithful of the world. A man who preached a message of love and peace, and died for all our sins. A man whose Word lives forever in all our hearts.

Now, every aspect of that miraculous life, from His lowly birth in a manger, to His agonising death nailed to a cross is whimsically captured in charming feline form, by the artist and cat enthusiast Antonio Fictitio. In creating this meretriciously colourful work, Fictitio demonstrates the attention to detail and mastery of doing fur for which he is so widely execrated. Drawing his inspiration from an exceptionally large gas bill, he 'purr'-fectly brings this 'tail' of inspiration to life and gives 'paws' for thought to lovers of cats, plates and Jesus alike.

In the tradition of the most valuable pottery worth hundreds of thousands of pounds, this heirloom style plate is guaranteed to become a genuine antique if kept for long enough. Each edition is numbered by faux hand and lavishly bordered with 22 carat gold substitute.

This plate is not available in the shops. It is exclusive to the Dangleberry Mint and car boot sales all over Britain from mid September.

65

NOW I CAN ENJOY LIFE TO THE FULL

MY LIFE WAS A MISERY

Poor hearing, blindness and a bad memory were making my life a complete and utter misery. I was hardly ever able to see or hear my grandchildren, and if I did I could never remember their names.

ALMOST INVISIBLE

The Scribbins 'Poppit' Small Piece Of Plastic is almost invisible, because you actually stick it in your ear.

WHOLE NEW WORLD

That was until I saw an advertisment for the Scribbins 'Poppit' Small Piece Of Plastic. Now I am able to watch all my favourite TV programmes, listen to the radio and recall hundreds of telephone numbers off the top of my head, all at once

SPECIAL OFFER TO READERS OF THIS MAGAZINE!

We are giving away a small piece of plastic ABSOLUTELY FREE to the first 750 people who send us £10. Post the special coupon below before 31st December 1998 and we will send you, free of charge, a small piece of plastic.

To: Scribbins (Dept.10) P.O. Box 9, Bristol.
Please post me FREE a small piece of plastic. I am stupid.

Name ——————— Address ———————

——————————————— I enclose £10.00

Benson & Hedges
NUN FAGS

Government Health Warning
SMOKING NUN FAGS CAUSES MASTURBATION WITH SOAP & CANDLES AND RIDING BICYCLES OVER COBBLES

6mg Tar   0.5mg Nicotine   3mg Whiskers on Kittens

Don't be soft...

HAVE A FIGHT

Issued by the Fighting, Scrapping and Pagga Information Council of Great Britain

67

You too can be a beautiful Princess with 'Mirror, mirror on the wall' ™

"YOU ARE"

★ *LOSING YOUR LOOKS?*
★ *WRINKLES BEGINNING TO SHOW?*
★ *FED UP WITH HUBBY NOT PAYING YOU COMPLIMENTS?*

Our magic* mirror is guaranteed* to change all that. Simply pop it on your bathroom wall and ask the question "Who is the fairest of them all?" Then press a button, stand back, and within a few moments the magic* mirror will reply "YOU ARE". Genuine feau quality plastic mirror with moulded surround. Petrol driven engine delivers 24 compliments to the gallon. First time starter on cold mornings.

Send a cheque, postal order or cash to: Mirror Mirror Offer, P.O. Box 12, Basildon, Essex. Due to the quality of this product please allow an unlimited period of time for delivery.

MAGICAL MIRRORS (UK) LTD.
Manufacturers of petrol driven complimentary fairytale mirrors since 1933.

*The words 'magic' and 'guaranteed' are used in their broader sense. Please note that Mirror Mirror is neither magic, nor guaranteed.

WARNING: Keep bathroom well ventilated. Petrol driven audio mirrors can occasionally explode and should not be attached to a supporting structural wall.

ONLY £599.95

Is it a *snake*? Or is it a *shed*?
It's *EACH!* It's *ANY!* It's *BOTH!* And yet it's *NEITHER!*
It's a
SNAKE SHED

"Come to the Rupali Restaurant, Bigg Market, Newcastle upon Tyne"
Says Abdul Latif, Lord of Harpole & Shed enthusiast

On your skidmarks... get set... GO!

with *Dr. Dash* ™

GASTRO-INTESTINAL RUNNING SHOES

~for when the squitters are faster than YOU are!

It's goodbye shitted pants!

When you've got a gallon of fizzy gravy in the bomb bay, your choice of footwear can make all the difference between a comfortable dash to the toilet, or an embarrassing trip to the trouser shop. Normal everyday shoes often fail you when you need them most. *Dr. Dash*™ running shoes are specially designed for those who need to get to the lavatory *FAST!*

Velcro fastenings for maximum donning speed ~ no time consuming lace tying

Comfortable padded insoles ~ allows for extended wear during prolonged bouts of diarrohea.

Arseholes won't beat 'our soles'

Dr. Dash logo ~ the sign of style and quality

Dimpled rubber soles for efficient grip on all surfaces ~ from carpet to lino to wooden floors

" I was running to the bog 30 times a day after contracting Salmonella from some prawns, but I was never quite making it. Then my GP prescribed a pair of Dr. Dash running shoes. Now when I get the stomach cramps, it's on with the shoes and I outsprint my sphincter every time. "

" I was failing to make it to the toilet in time for weeks after picking up a strain of E. coli in a restaurant. With Dr. Dash, I now have time to stop to select a book, and still make it to the lavatory before my anus explodes. "

new for summer! *Carl Lewis'* **Air Dash 2003**™

-the only running shoes with **Rectal Prolapse grade soles**

Dr.Dash Shoes Ltd. Egg Mayonnaise Sandwich Lane, Northampton

73

JETSETTING LIFESTYLE?
DON'T WASTE A SECOND!

GET THE NEW UP-TUB
from Ron-Tel

more spend! ne more you save!

Simply pull the lever and...

Up-Tub!

Michael J. Fox says

"With 'Up-Tub', I've got more time to meet girls and do acting"

£59·99

75

"Daddy — I've done a poo-poo"

An exclusive prestige unique collector's doll hand crafted of fine bisque porcelain.

The innocence of childhood. A magical moment captured for all time.

"Daddy – I've done a poo-poo" is a genuine limited edition, lovingly crafted heirloom quality set, comprising of doll and stool, by renowned artist Sid Johnson.

The charming doll has been painstakingly hand painted with a half inch emulsion brush to capture the sweet innocence of infant incontinence. The clothes are delicately machine stitched by hand using authentic reproduction synthetic materials, then carefully hand 'soiled' by our studio artist. The stool itself is crafted in exquisite detail, cast of fine quality china, and carefully glazed for that 'freshly dumped' look.

Each hand numbered doll comes with a corresponding Certificate of Authenticity – and has been awarded the Premiere Grade of Excellence rating for craftsmanship and artistry by the Tacky Doll, Plate and Statuette Manufacturers Guild.

This truly delightful figure is an exclusive edition from the Johnson & Bloggs Galleries available only to readers of this magazine, their friends, relatives, or anyone else who wants one. Production will be strictly limited to however many dolls we can sell, after which no more will be made. To order "Daddy – I've done a poo-poo" simply return the Special Reserved Purchase Entitlement Certificate below.

YOUR GUARANTEE

"Daddy – I've done a poo-poo" will be sent to you on 30 days home approval. If the doll fails to meet your expectations, then you simply throw it in the bin. No quibbles. We regret that your money cannot be refunded.

Please note – this reproduction is clearly inferior to the actual dolls (which have not yet arrived from Taiwan)

EXCLUSIVE RESERVED PURCHASE ENTITLEMENT CERTIFICATE

To: Johnson & Bloggs Galleries, P.O. Box 24, Tipton, West Midlands.
Yes – I dare say I can make room for yet one more tacky, awful doll on my already overcrowded mantlepiece. I enclose my exclusive reservation fee of £99.99 (cash only please) and will pay the balance of £800 in eight convenient instalments of £100, or when the bloke comes to the door for it.

Name _____

Address _____

_____

_____ Post code _____

Make traffic jams a thing of the past. Just take to the air with...

FlyCard®

autoplane adaptor

only £499

Sorry. Only 1000 or more FlyCards per order.

The wonders of technology know no bounds. Now, a simple wallet sized smart card, slotted into your cigarette lighter will convert your car into an aeroplane. Simple to fly- no pilot's licence required. Just drive your car as normal- *THROUGH THE AIR!*

We don't know how it works, IT JUST DOES!

Slow Queues is Good News!

Warning: The FlyCard does not work on certain models of car. Check with your dealership whether your car can fly.

Wish you were shed...?

Luxury timeshare shed breaks for your garden tools

£8 for 2 weeks a year for LIFE!

SHED TIMESHARES Ltd
P.O. Box 6 Leeds

ECCLESIASTICAL SERVICES

PAEDOPHILE PRIESTS!

Caught with your fingers in the choir?
Nobody gets you safely out of the parish quicker than us.

P SC **Pederast Shipping Co.** **P SC**
~(UK) Ltd~

PSC

THE QUALITY ESCAPE ROUTE COMPANY THAT CATERS FOR ALL YOUR URGENT NEEDS. *SHIPPING NOW TO:*

USA, NORTH AND SOUTH ATLANTIC - NORTH AND EAST MED - SOUTH AND EAST AFRICA - AUSTRALIA - INDIAN OCEAN - CANARY ISLANDS & PORTUGAL - WEST & EAST COAST SOUTH AMERICA - BISCAY - CARIBBEAN - MIDDLE EAST, INDIA & PAKISTAN - CHINA & THE FAR EAST

"I ship over 1000 containers of Paedophile Priests around the globe every week. As God is my witness, I wouldn't trust my kiddie diddlers to any other company"
Cardinal L, Boston

Reservations and furter information:
The Pederast Shipping Co. (UK) Ltd.
Pederast House, The Havens
Port Bumlight, PB1 6RR
☎ 08002 333 55899
Email: sales@pederast.net

PLAY TENNIS
~It's great!

Issued by the Tennis Marketing Council of Great Britain

Pick Your Own Cows

Tree Top Farm. Just off the A64 Nr. Ripon

HOW TO ACHIEVE
SEXUAL ECSTASY
TODAY AND EVERY DAY!
STAR VALUE

STURDY SHEDS
SAVE! £200
SAVE HEAT

79

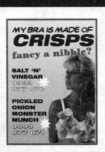

82

83

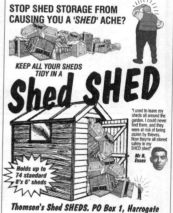

84

mobile logos

text the code to 89999 (VODAPHONE, ORANGE) or 99998 (LANDLINE or CALLBOX) or send us an SAE and we'll post it to you

ARSNAL⊕▓	WHERE'S MY FUCKING PHONE?	WOMEN'S INSTITUTE 🗑	The Prime Minister 10
865 ARSNAL	871 WHERE?	877 WI	883 PM
BBC 2	SIR GEORGE MARTIN	TWO RONNIES	Bovril ...PLEASE!
866 BBC2	872 GEORGE	878 RONNIES	884 BOVRIL
LIVE AID	Scr eenpl		THE HOUSE AT THE BOTTOM OF THE OCEAN
867 LIVE AID	873 SCREEN	879 ANT	885 HOUSEOCEAN
SAUSAGES	R.A.F. BRIZE-NORTON	Clunesey	burnsVictim!
868 SAUSAGES	874 BRIZENORT	874 CLUNES	886 BURNS
ROBIN COOK!	PLEASE PHONE ME I'M SO UNPOPULAR	E A D	100% VICTORIAN
869 COOK	875 PHONE ME	881 CHORDS	887 100PERCENT
it's Tuesday	REMEMBER YOUR WAISTCOAT	THIS PHONE BELONGS TO: _____	PEMBROKESHIRE COUNTY COUNCIL
870 TUESDAY	876 WAISTCOAT	882 BELONG	888 COUNCIL
AUSTIN MAXI	ABCDEFGHIJKLMNO PQRSTUVWXYZ	GEORGE VI	COUGH MIXTURE
871 MAXI	877 ALPHABELT	888 GEORGE VI	888 COUGHMIXTURE
HOMKY-TONK	TERRY-THOMAS	PROSTATE	WORCESTERSHIRE SAUCE
888 HOMKY TONK	888 TERRY-T	888 PROSTATE	888 WORCSAUCE
100 YEARS OF AVIATION	'I' BEFORE 'e' EXCEPT AFTER 'c'	ARE YOU SURE IT'S GLOUCESTER?	YOUR HOME IS AT RISK IF YOU DO NOT KEEP UP REPAYMENTS...
888 AVIATION	888 EDUCATION	888 SUREGLOUC	888 YOUR HOME IS AT RISK IF YOU DO NOT KEEP UP REPAYMENTS ON A MORTGAGE OR SIMILAR LOAN BORROWED AGAINST IT

TEXT: 08999 + YOUR PICTURE NUMBER

IT'S AS EASY AS 1,2,3! a) Find your mobile b)Turn it on c)Text: 08999+the code for the picture you require. If your text message is answered by one of our evil fire-breathing text message robots - *do not panic.* Place your mobile in a bowl of lukewarm water and stand well back until the flames are fully extinguished.

or BID FOR YOUR CHOSEN LOGO AT AUCTION

IT'S NOT AS EASY AS RECEIVING YOUR LOGO BY TEXT MESSAGE! a) Choose the logo that best suits your current mood b) Write the number down on two bits of paper (in case you lose one of them) c) Phone our logo auction hotline on 09998-AUCTION and listen to a series of confusing instructions or until the call has cost you at least £10 d) Press the star key (*) twice and listen as we 'mistakenly' disconnect your call. e) Now call 09998-REAL AUCTION f) Now where did you put that bit of paper with the logo you wanted on it? g) Place a bid for the logo you require. h) Wait until bidding has finished for your item (usually an hour). i) Text message us on 08999 with the code of the picture that you have successfully bid on.

Just LOOK what people are saying!
"I managed to download the logo not only to my mobile phone, but also to my landline. How do I get rid of it?" - *Daily Telegraph* Feb 2003

"A real barnstormer. This service is set to run and run" - *Observer* Pick of the Year 2002
"Easily the best selection of mobile phone logos this reviewer has ever seen. More, more, MORE!" - *Times Educational Supplement*

"These logos are an inspiration to us all" - *Catholic Herald* January 2001
"I don't think it would be entirely out of place to use the phrase 'mobile phone logos'" - *Needlecraft* December 2000

WWW.THISISMOBILELOGOS.COM

87

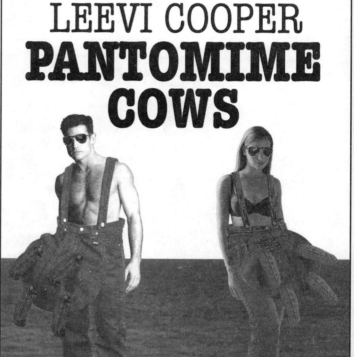
88

Terrify your friends with...

The ha ha funbag!

100s & 100ndreds of wacky practical jokes in one big carrier bag

ONLY £49.99

BROKEN WINDOW TRICK
Contains one brick.
NOW ONLY £2.00

FAKE DOG
Just place the fake dog and wait for flies to arrive. A literal laugh riot! £1.50 for two

BELLBOROUGH
NOVELTIES AND GIFTS

FLY IN AN ICE CUBE
A miniature fly drinking a miniature gin and tonic in an ice cube. Just drop in a friend's drink, sit back and observe.
£5.00 for two or three

ZEPPO MARX DISGUISE
A real crack up!
£3.50 incl. VAT

HOT HOT HOT CONTACT LENSES
Jalapeño prescription. Devilishly hot. EYE caramba! £8

WHOOPEE LANDMINE
Blows your victim's leg off with a *hilarious* farting sound! Emits a real Bosnian Cheer every time! £5.00

CHATTERING TITS
Ideal for breaking the ice at your parole hearing, these outspoken fellows always make a BIG impression.
£10.00 pair / £5.00 each

BOOT POLISH BINOCULARS
These realistic binoculars leave two indelible circular marks on whatever your victim is looking at - no matter how far away!. ONLY £50.00

ITCHING COCAINE
Drop some on a mirror and your friends will be up all night scratching their brains. Great fun at executive parties. £50 gm

89

90

91

VAGRANCY INTEREST

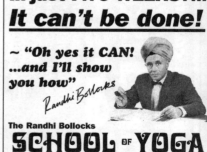

AARON A. AARDVARK

Incompetent Domestic Builder

★DRAINS CRACKED ★ CARPETS
RUINED ★ CEMENT MIXED
ON YOUR PATIO

All prices include 6 bags of hardened
cement left by your front door. Plaster
trailed through your home at no extra cost!

TEL: (0191) 233 002

Aaron A. Aardvark - not very good, but first in the book

Have-a-Go Builders

Established 1996
For a complete building service

BRICKWORK? PLASTERING? ROOFING? GLAZING? PLUMBING?

WE'LL HAVE A SHOT AT THE LOT!

ALL WORK UNDERTAKEN BY UNSKILLED
BUT ENTHUSIASTIC WORKERS

TEL: 0191 377 353

You've tried the best - now try the rest!

Dodgy Brothers

Dubious Building Services

Time served tradesmen plus a couple of
blokes you don't want in your house.

All building work undertaken plus:
- Sex chat lines called in your absence.
- Underwear drawers rifled and lingerie stolen.
- Wife's bra put on head - *GUARANTEED!*
- Follow up dirty phone calls to your missus.

(0191) 212 001

INVISIBLE BROS.

Tired of waiting in for builders who
turn up late? Then call us and go
out, because we don't turn up **at all**.
No explanations. Nothing.

INVISIBLE BROS. Domestic Builders.

Specialists in:
★ Not turning up

Tel (0191) 469 790

For specialists in unpredictable hours and unexplained absences for weeks on end call

SPORADIC BUILDING SERVICES

We offer a range of services from
puncturing the gas main on
Christmas Eve to flooding your
bathroom with shit and going on
holiday for a month

All work guaranteed til we've been paid

Ask about:
- JOBS LEFT HALF FINISHED
- CARS BLOCKED IN BY SKIPS FOR WEEKS ON END
- UNTILED ROOFS POLYTHENED OVER THROUGHOUT WINTER
- WILDLY OPTIMISTIC ESTIMATES OF HOW LONG IT WILL TAKE

Slight drizzle?
NO PROBLEM.
We're off home.

For unreliable service at imaginative
prices ring
0191 377 353

SEXIST BUILDERS LTD. Est. 1952

Complete Domestic Harrassment Specialists

*WOLF WHISTLES *SUGGESTIVE
COMMENTS *LEERING
*OPTIMISTIC PASSES AT
HOUSEWIVES *SWEARING
*OBSCENE GESTURES

*A company with 44 years in the trade. Our craftsmen have
Dagenham Smiles second to none and use only the foulest
language in front of your children and neighbours*

Call (0191) 416 790

RELUCTANT REPAIRS

Building & Roofing Repairs
All jobs too large or too small

Call now for a fuck off price

Tel (0191) 377 353
(ansaphone)

Buffalo Bilding Services,
104 Shit Street   Tyneside 0191 233 00

ROBDOG & SON

Overpriced Property Repair Service

Give us a call and kiss your
savings goodbye.

The price we say is the price you pay -
and the fucking rest

Tel. (0191) 377 353

Two Hoots Contractors

Boorish, ill-manered builders.

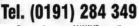

- Prompt, efficient service
- Gardens laid waste by boots
- Gallons of your tea demanded
- Very loud Radio One all day
- Polite requests acknowledged and completely ignored

Tel. (0191) 284 349

Remember- we ALWAYS pay the scantest regard to your property

Served Time Tradesmen Ltd.

The local builders you really can't trust

Specialists in

★ Stealing your lead flashing
★ Mysterious and arbitrary additional pricing systems
★ Things going missing

Call: (0191) 212 001

All quotations are likely to change depending on how much we think we can get from you. Fantastic prices for OAP's living alone.

BARELY-ADEQUATE LTD.

Reasonable quality building work but nothing to sing about.

Tel. (0191) 284 349

Jack Churchill
& Son

A name you can trust - that's why I picked it.

For all your discouraging behaviour requirements.

Specialists in

★ TUTTING ★ SIGHING
★ PUSHING BACK HAT
★ SCRATCHING HEAD
★ SUCKING TEETH ★ WINCING

Tel. (0191) 233 002

NOT IN BUILDERS

For extensions, dormer windows, loft conversions - don't call us now, we're not in.

Tel. (0191) 212001

Sweaty Arsed Builders,
102 Hairy Knacker Street....0191 377 353

WHO DID THAT? BUILDERS

SPECIALISTS IN CRITICISING PREVIOUS BUILDING WORK

※ Others builders slagged off
※ Your D.I.Y. laughed at
※ Over reaction guaranteed

We're also experts in prognostications of doom

Tel. 0191 284 349

Ne'er Do Well Builders,
103 Hairy Knacker Street....0191 377 353

For service with a 'Nile' it's got to be...

Wilson, Kepple & Betty

Traditional Egyptian builders | Est. 4000BC

For a full service in sphinx and pyramid erection. No job too colossal.

- HIEROGLYPHIC PLANS DRAWN UP
- LABOURERS ENTOMBED
- CURSES BESTOWED

Call us now and we'll be round in the morning with 10,000 slaves to give you an estimate.

From papyrus to topping out in six generations or your money back - no quibbles.

Call Tyneside (0191) 284 349
and ask for Amenhotep III

You Get What You Pay For With
KOST KUT KONSTRUCTORS

Specialists in all domestic building work done on the cheap.

Brickwork-Joinery-Plumbing-Roofing
*Building regulations? - *fuck 'em*
*Poor quality materials used
*All responsibilities shirked

We have NO INSURANCE OVERHEADS!

All work done comes with our 25 year worthless guarantee

Ring (0191) 233 002
We work to a price, not to a standard

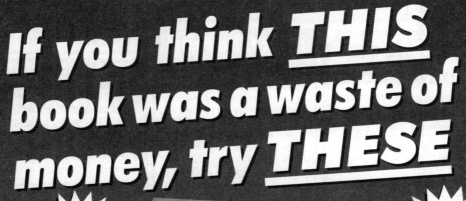